WKFM 2000
Nicole
Eden
Zach
Austin
Sandra

MEET THE MISSIONARY

Meet the Missionary

Written by Mark Weinrich

Illustrated by Brenda Wintermyer (Step One Design)

Meet the Missionary is a story in the *Missionary—That's Me!* series

CHRISTIAN PUBLICATIONS / Camp Hill, Pennsylvania

The mark of vibrant faith

Christian Publications
3825 Hartzdale Drive, Camp Hill, PA 17011

ISBN: 0-87509-517-8
Printed in the United States of America

93 94 95 96 97 5 4 3 2 1

CHILE
PERU
MISSIONARY

I can't wait until the missionary comes. It's my favorite time of the year. Every year before the missionary comes, we decorate our church with brightly colored posters, flags, maps and curios. Curios are special items like clothing, pictures or animal skins from other countries.

"We're all ready, Mommy. Now the missionary party can begin," I said excitedly.

Mother laughed. "The 'missionary party' is called a missionary convention or conference," she said.

When the missionary—Mr. Zimmer was his name—came for the missionary convention this year, he stayed at our house. Often he told stories about the country he lives in and prayed with us before we went to bed, just like my mom and dad do.

I slept in my brother Jeremy's room so Mr. Zimmer could sleep in my room.

When Mr. Zimmer came, Mom made a cake shaped like the country where he lives. It's like an extra special birthday cake.

"Can I put the candles on?" I asked.

"Not yet," she smiled and said, "You must listen during church and tell me how many people Mr. Zimmer says came to know Jesus last year."

During the missionary conference we had a parade. Instead of marching down the street, we marched down the aisle in Sunday school and church carrying big flags and wearing beautiful costumes from different lands.

As we marched, Mr. Zimmer held the head of a curio he brought. It was the skin of a giant snake called a python. He let me hold the tail while the other kids marched between us. Jeremy followed us playing a funny kind of drum.

In Sunday school Mr. Zimmer taught us the song, "Jesus Loves Me" in the language of the people where he lives.

"Will you sing it with me in church?" he asked.

"Yes," we said gladly and practiced again.

He also told us exciting stories about the snake and the drum. I listened closely so I could find out how many candles we needed for the special birthday cake.

Then our Sunday school teacher put a box with balloons on it at the other end of the room. The missionary took out something long and narrow and slipped off its long cover. It was a blowgun!

Aiming at the balloon, he took a sharp dart and blew it through the gun. "POP!" The dart burst the balloon.

"Wow!" we exclaimed.

"Would you all like to try?" the missionary asked.

You bet we did. We all jumped up, eager to take a turn using the blowgun. Some of us even popped a balloon!

Finally it was time to sing our special song in church. We sang it just the way the missionary taught us. I looked at Mr. Zimmer and saw that he had tears in his eyes. I wondered why. *Had we made him sad?* I listened carefully as he spoke.

"There was a time when no one in our country sang 'Jesus Loves Me' the way the children did this morning. In Matthew 28, Jesus told us to go into all the world and preach the gospel. That is why missionaries have gone to this country. Now thousands of our people know about Jesus and His love, and they can sing 'Jesus Loves Me.'"

Tears ran down Mr. Zimmer's face. I understood now. They were tears of joy.

Mr. Zimmer was happy because so many people had learned about Jesus.

"In fact," he continued, "over 100 people trusted Jesus as their Savior last year."

"Amen." everyone said.

"Over 100," I whispered to myself. Mommy and Daddy looked at me and smiled. They knew what I was thinking.

CLICK!
CLICK!

That evening Mr. Zimmer showed slides of his country. There was one slide that showed a missionary with the big python just after it had been killed near his house.

I thought the slides were neat, but I couldn't wait to help mother with the cake. I was so excited, it was hard to sit still.

After the service, Mom and I rushed to the church kitchen. Finally it was time to make our big surprise.

"Mom, Mr. Zimmer said over 100 people trusted Jesus as their Savior. Should we put 101 candles on the cake?" I asked.

"Yes," Mother replied with a big smile.

We took the big cake to the fellowship hall. Everyone gathered around it. When the missionary and all the children saw the cake, they were so surprised.

"Is it your birthday?" someone asked Mr. Zimmer.

"Nobody could be *that* old!" Jeremy announced.

Laughing, our pastor said, "We're celebrating the spiritual birthdays of over 100 people. We're rejoicing like the angels do in heaven when someone trusts Jesus as Savior."

"Hey kids, why don't you help me blow out the candles," Mr. Zimmer said.

Leaning forward, we blew out the candles. We laughed and clapped as a little cloud of smoke rose to the ceiling.

Then Pastor Miller prayed. "Dear Lord, use Mr. Zimmer and his family to lead many more people to trust in Jesus."

Everyone was happy. Some people even had happy tears in their eyes. I thought it was the *best* birthday party ever!

ABOUT THE AUTHOR

Mark Weinrich is the pastor of Fellowship Alliance Church. He and his wife Lucy live in Truth or Consequences, New Mexico with their children Amie and Matthew. Mark is a prolific writer, having published more than 280 articles and poems in over 75 publications.

Hey Kids!

If you enjoyed *Meet the Missionary* why not read other books in the *Missionary—That's Me!* series. And if you enjoy reading stories about missions and missionaries, Christian Publications has two other series available for children: a series of missionary biographies, *The Junior Jaffray Collection of Missionary Stories*; and four books of true stories from mission fields around the world, *Bare, Beautiful Feet*, *A Happy Day for Ramona*, *The Pink and Green Church* and *The Potato Story*.